SAVING CECELIA

CERRA DREEMSTAR

WingSpan Press

Dedicated to Jef. This was made so you and your children will inherit a better earth. Thank you for always believing in me.

And to Jeannie W. who inspired me to create this in the first place.

Proceeds from this book go to a trustworthy foundation to preserve the rainforest.

Published in the United States and the United Kingdom by WingSpan Press, Livermore, CA

The WingSpan name, logo and colophon are the trademarks of WingSpan Publishing.

ISBN 978-1-59594-962-2

Second edition 2020

Printed in the United States of America

www.wingspanpress.com

Library of Congress Control Number: 2020908810

1 2 3 4 5 6 7 8 9 10

Salutations! I'm Victor, the Boa Constrictor. I would like to share a story with you today, because our time has come. We — the animals of the earth — are in great need from the human beings of the earth. (That's all of you reading my tale. No, not the "other end of me" tail but the story I'm about to tell you.)

First let's go on a little trip. We'll sail to a place called South America. It's very scenic there, where there are more trees and plants than you or I can count. These places with so many trees and plants are called Rain Forests.

There's quite a lot of rain and wetness there, which all the plants and animals love. Did I mention animals? Yes, yes, I did, didn't I? There are many fascinating animals in the Rain Forest. I couldn't possibly tell you about each and every one of them today, but, I can tell you about a few of them right now.

South America

I have a very good friend that lives with me in the Rain Forest. Her name is "Cecelia". (Such a superb name, don't you think?) Well, Cecelia is a 3-Toed Sloth. Do you know what a Sloth is? I bet you probably do, but I enjoy describing her so much, that I simply must do so.

Cecelia is a large creature with two arms and two legs, like a monkey, but with one big difference. She hangs upside down from branches all her life. She has claws, like big hooks, that hang on to the branches. Whereas monkeys like to jump around very quickly, Cecelia moves so, so, so slow. So slow, that you can barely see her move. She rarely goes on the ground, because she cannot walk well on the ground. She is very sure footed in the trees, though. What amazes me about my Cecelia, is she is a marvelous swimmer. Slow, but marvelous. (She can even hold her breath for a very long time.)

Three-Toed Sloth

Cecelia and I are so lucky. We live in a paradise. Right where she hangs, she has all the fruit and leafs she wants to eat. And because she only eats fruit and leaves, that makes her an herbivore. But guess what? She eats slowly too. Cecelia's favorite leaves are from the Cecropia Tree.

Speaking of eating, you all know that some animals eat other animals, to live, don't you? These animals that eat other animals are called carnivores. Since Cecelia moves so slow, it would be very easy for the carnivores to eat her, wouldn't it? Yes, this is true, they do want to. But Cecelia has things that protect her. One, is that she hangs upside down, it's hard for most of them to get to her. Second, is that she moves so slowly, they never see her move. Third, sometimes she strikes at them with her hook claws and can scare them away. But the fourth thing and the strangest thing, is that in her thick, long fur grows a green algae which makes her look green.

This green look to Cecelia makes her the same color as the trees she lives in, making it harder for her to be seen. When an animal looks like the place it's living in, this is called camouflage.

Remember those carnivores? Carnivores are sometimes called predators. One of the predators that makes life in Cecelia's world so dangerous is the Giant Harpy. A Giant Harpy is the biggest, meanest, most ferocious Eagle in the whole world! Just thinking about him makes shivers go up and down the over 200 bones in my spine!! We all call him "Horrible". "Horrible Harpy". This guy can fly as fast as a car in and out of the tree tops trying to grab a monkey or two. So, sometimes Cecelia is in grave danger, because ol' Horrible can even fly upside down!

Giant Harpy

Cecelia, on the other hand, has some very nice friends. Actually, these friends are quite interesting and I think you might like to hear about them. One of them is a Marmosa. "Mamey", the Marmosa, also lives up in the trees. She eats fruit and hunts insects. Mamey is also known as a "mouse opossum". Other opossums play dead when they get scared and that tricks other animals into leaving them alone. But not Mamey! She'll stand right up to even a predator. She's not scared. The reason this is so amazing is because she is no bigger than a human thumb! That's why she's called a mouse opossum.

Marmosa

Mamey has other opossum cousins that are bigger than her. "Kinjee" the Kinkajou is one of them. Kinjee has a long tail that holds onto the branches like another hand would. This kind of tail is called a prehensile tail. Kinjee looks like a silly clown hanging upside down by her tail.

Kinkajou

In the Rain Forest, and another one of Cecelia's buddies, lives the largest rodent in the world. That happens to be "Clara" the Capybara. Her feet are webbed just like a duck's feet are. These webbed feet help her swim most of the time. When she's not swimming, she's walking on top of muddy, swampy ground and those feet keep her from sinking down into it. I guess I'm pretty lucky she's an herbivore because she's big enough to eat me!

Capybara

The friend of Cecelia's that keeps us all very entertained, is a baby Hoatzin Bird. We call him "Haphazard". He has a tiny claw on the end of his wings. Right after he hatches, he starts climbing around from branch to branch, hanging on with those little claws. He is so clumsy! He tries to hang on with the wing claw, his feet and even his beak, but he still falls. When he grows up, he's still clumsy. He'll fly for a short distance and then crash right into the ground. It is so funny to watch.

Hoatzin Bird

We have another friend who keeps us highly amused. Our funny, fast-footed friend, "Bezerk" is a Basilisk Lizard. He looks so funny because he looks just like a tiny dinosaur. But what's so funny about him is that he will run on top of water without sinking and he gets going so fast that he ends up standing up and running on two legs! We never get tired of watching him do this little water trick of his. It is quite a sight to see.

Basilisk Lizard

There is a most striking looking creature that lives here in our forest. This is the Ocelot.

"Ozzley", as we call him, has beautiful stripes and spots like his distant cousin, the leopard. It's just that Ozzley is about the same size as your pet cats at home. A leopard is a very large cat that you would not want to tangle with.

Ocelot

Our home in the Rain Forest is always like an exquisite painting of a lovely spot in the world. When you have brightly colored Tanager Birds around you, like "Tango" here, it makes everything even more beautiful with all the colors of the rainbow surrounding you. As with many of the birds here, his colors are radiant and quite a sight to behold.

Tanager Bird

I, too, have a special friend. "Cookie", is a Boa Constrictor, like me, only Cookie is a Cook's Boa. Isn't she pretty? She's not a poisonous snake, but she will give you a big squeeze if you get her riled up. That's why we are called "constrictors". We constrict or "squeeze" our food before we eat it. Don't be afraid, though. We are predators, too, but not all predators are vicious.

Cook's Boa

The last little creature I'm going to tell you about today is another character we enjoy here in the forest. He is a very small monkey.

That's why he's called a Squirrel Monkey. He would fit nicely in your lap. What's interesting about "Skip", is that his tail is longer than his whole body. But, he cannot use it to hold on to the branches like the Kinkajou can with its prehensile tail. Skip runs around the tops of the trees all of his life with about a hundred other Squirrel Monkeys. They like to stay in large groups like that. That's a big family.

Squirrel Monkey

I prefer to be alone, but that's what makes us all so fascinating is that we're all different. Just like all of you humans. You are all very different and a very fascinating species to me.

And because of who you are, that's why I told you this story today. The reason for my story was for you to come to know Cecelia and how special she and the other animals of the forest are.

Every day large areas of our beautiful forest are cut down and destroyed by human beings who want to use the land for other uses. When the forest dies, so do we.

I want you to remember who we are so that you can use your superior brains to figure out ways to end the destruction of our homes here. Please help us live. Save our forest. Save us……….Save Cecelia.

www.ingramcontent.com/pod-product-compliance
Lightning Source LLC
Chambersburg PA
CBHW042007080426
42733CB00003B/37